WONDERS
OF NATURAL
NEW ZEALAND

David Bateman

Published in 2007 by David Bateman Ltd,

30 Tarndale Grove, Albany, Auckland, New Zealand

ISBN 978-1-86953-686-2

Design: Alice Bell

Printed in China through Colorcraft Ltd., Hong Kong

Right: Nikau palms, Banks Peninsula, Christchurch.

Contents

Left: Mt Tasman, 3,497 m, with Fox Glacier to the left.

NEW ZEALAND

North Island

South Island

The Picturesque North

The Volcanic Heart

North to South

Big Country

The Deep South

Cape Reinga

Ninety Mile Beach

BAY OF ISLANDS

Waipoua Forest

WHANGAREI

Goat Island Marine Reserve

Tiritiri Matangi

HAURAKI GULF

Muriwai

Rangitoto

Piha

AUCKLAND

Miranda

Coromandel

Waikato River

Hauraki Plains

TAURANGA

White Island

HAMILTON

Otorohanga

Waitomo

ROTORUA

WHAKATANE

Urewera National Park

NEW PLYMOUTH

Whanganui River Journey

L Taupo

Huka Falls

Tongariro Crossing

Tongariro National Park

Lake Waikaremoana Track

Taranaki

Egmont National Park

Whanganui National Park

Mt Ruapehu

NAPIER

WANGANUI

Cape Kidnappers

Mt Bruce National Wildlife Centre

Farewell Spit

Abel Tasman National Park

Kapiti Island

Castlepoint

Heaphy Track

Kahurangi National Park

Abel Tasman Coastal Track

Karori Sanctuary

WELLINGTON

NELSON

PICTON

COOK STRAIT

Cape Foulwind

Paparoa National Park

Nelson Lakes National Park

Punakaiki

Kaikoura

Arthur's Pass National Park

Westland/ Tai Poutini National Park

CHRISTCHURCH

Banks Peninsula

Okarito

Fox and Franz Josef Glaciers

Mt Cook National Park

Akaroa Harbour

Haast Pass

Twizel

Mt Aspiring National Park

Milford Sound

Routeburn Track

OAMARU

QUEENSTOWN

L Wakatipu

Kepler Track

Moeraki

Fiordland National Park

Te Anau

Otago Peninsula

DUNEDIN

INVERCARGILL

The Catlins

Rakiura National Park

Oban

STEWART ISLAND

Introduction

Situated on the Pacific rim's 'ring of fire', New Zealand is a land experiencing constant change. From the raw landscape of Tongariro National Park to the older forested volcanic cones of Coromandel and Northland the evidence of upheaval is obvious. The eruptions of Mt Ruapehu in the 1990s and White Island more recently, along with the spectacular geothermal features of the central North Island, are reminders that the land is subject to dramatic upheaval.

The South Island's landscape also owes much to movements of the earth's crust. The Southern Alps are being pushed up by a collision of the Pacific and Australian plates, rising at a rate of 10–20 mm per year, and earthquakes regularly rock both main islands along a string of fault lines.

However, despite the constant renewal of the landscape, New Zealand is home to some ancient forms of life. Some of the country's forests have changed little since dinosaurs wandered through them, and the tuatara, a reptile of those times, can still be found on some of New Zealand's offshore islands.

For the last 80 million years New Zealand has been isolated from the world, allowing the evolution of many plants and animals unique to this country. At a time when mammals dominated much of the planet, New Zealand's only terrestrial mammals were bats. This allowed birds and insects to fill a range of niches which gave the country an unusual and highly endemic fauna. The flora is just as diverse, largely due to the country's geographic isolation and equable climate.

Top left: Kaka, the large forest parrot.
Top right: Punakaiki, on the west coast of the South Island.

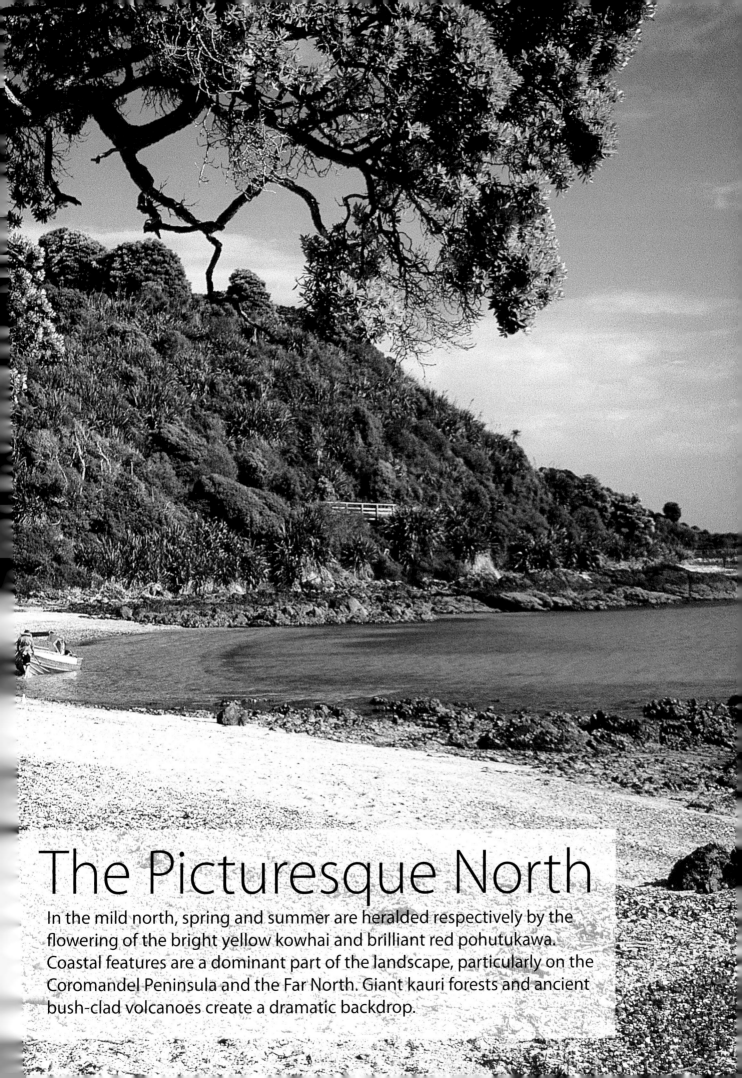

The Picturesque North

In the mild north, spring and summer are heralded respectively by the flowering of the bright yellow kowhai and brilliant red pohutukawa. Coastal features are a dominant part of the landscape, particularly on the Coromandel Peninsula and the Far North. Giant kauri forests and ancient bush-clad volcanoes create a dramatic backdrop.

Northland

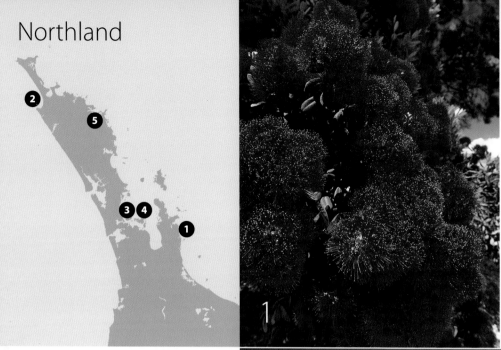

1 Its profusion of bright red flowers in December and January has led the **pohutukawa** to be known as the New Zealand Christmas tree. Clinging to the coastlines of Northland and **Coromandel**, these trees are often alive with nectar-feeding insects and birds such as the glossy black tui.

2 Ninety Mile Beach, though nearer 60 miles (100 km) in actual length, disappears into the distance, flanked by breaking waves and large sand dunes. The beach acts as a scenic highway for visitors to Cape Reinga, where the Pacific Ocean meets the Tasman Sea.

3 Tiritiri Matangi Island is one of many wildlife sanctuaries around the country with easy access for visitors. Home to rare native birds such as saddlebacks and kiwi, sanctuaries such as this provide a glimpse of the abundant birdlife that once made New Zealand's forests ring with birdsong.

4 Saddlebacks (tieke) almost became extinct in the early 1900s, but they survived on one small island to become a gem among New Zealand's birdlife. Full of character, this chatty bird still delights visitors to a number of islands such as **Tiritiri Matangi** in the Hauraki Gulf.

5

4

5 The wonderfully sheltered inlets and bays of the **Bay of Islands** are home to around 150 islands protected by Cape Brett peninsula in the east. A number of these islands are conservation reserves abundant in birds and marine life. With its many secluded anchorages, the area is a mecca for sailors while fishermen chase after big game fish, such as marlin, in deeper waters .

6 New Zealand's first 'no take' marine reserve was established in 1975 at Goat Island, and others, such as this one at the **Poor Knights Islands**, have since been formed. Here, fish that are commonly caught and eaten are able to grow old and large – a real spectacle when you're in the water with them.

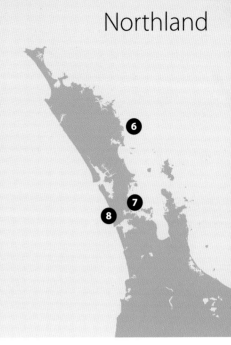

8 So rarely these days do we see wildlife in large numbers that the gathering of thousands of **gannets** (takapu) at their breeding colonies, such as at **Muriwai**, is a truly amazing sight. The complex social interaction between male and female, and between the pairs jostling for nesting space, provides hours of fascinating viewing.

7 Around 20 million years ago the raw material for these **sedimentary rocks** was eroded from long-vanished mountains and laid in neat layers on the sea floor. A huge submarine landslide then folded them like play dough and, now thrust up again, the wave action has exposed these wonderful patterns on the **Whangaparaoa Peninsula**.

Northland

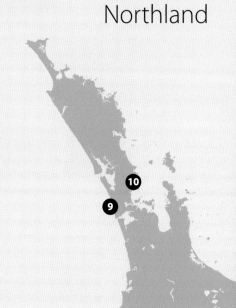

9 The black sands of the North Island's **west coast beaches** originate in the volcanoes of Taranaki and the central plateau, and are moved north by ocean currents to Auckland beaches such as **Piha** and Muriwai. Burning hot on the feet in summer, they are the raw material for the country's iron production.

10 The **kowhai** tree boasts New Zealand's national flower. It grows throughout the country, largely along forest margins and riverbanks – the region from Waiwera to Warkworth is known as the **Kowhai Coast**. Trees flower between July and October (earliest in the warmer north) and the spectacular display attracts a multitude of nectar-feeding birds, such as the **tui** (pictured here) and the melodic bellbird.

10

Northland

11 Rangitoto Island in the Hauraki Gulf appeared only about 600 years ago, the youngest of almost 50 volcanoes that have erupted in the Auckland area in the last 150,000 years. It is only in the last century that the sharp scoria slopes have become cloaked in a forest of pohutukawa.

12 The extensive **mangrove forests** that line the harbours of the north, seen here at **Waitangi Estuary**, slowly diminish further south where temperatures become too cool for them. These highly fertile mangrove ecosystems shelter a vast array of life and are an important nursery for the young of many fish species.

13 The unusually elongated snout of the **giraffe weevil** (tuwhipapa) gives this insect a distinctive appearance. The larvae of this weevil lives as a borer in forest trees throughout New Zealand, including the **Waipoua** kauri forest, and only when it emerges does the snout of the male straighten to such an impressive length.

14 At 51 m tall, with a girth of 14 m, the 1200-year-old **Tane Mahuta** in **Waipoua Forest** is the largest surviving kauri. These forest giants once covered much of northern New Zealand, including the Coromandel Peninsula, but were felled for their valuable timber.

15 New Zealand has 11 recorded species of dolphin, though not all are as familiar or interactive as this **common dolphin** (aihe) in the sheltered **Hauraki Gulf**. Fifty-one species of marine mammal have been recorded in New Zealand waters, more than any other country.

15

16

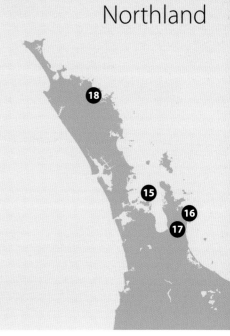

17

17 The Pinnacles, one of many outcrops of volcanic rock that stand out along the Coromandel Range, are a jagged rib of rhyolite in the upper Kauaeranga Valley near Thames. The range was volcanically active about eight million years ago, and since then the softer surrounding rocks have eroded deeply, creating this dramatic landscape.

18 Nocturnal, whiskered, brown and snuffling – this sounds like the description of a small mammal, but then the **kiwi** is an unusual bird. Among their many distinctive features, they are the only birds to have nostrils at the tips of their beaks. There are small mainland populations throughout the country, including near **Kerikeri** in Northland.

16 Cathedral Cove, named for the grand arch that passes through the headland from Mare's Leg Cove, is only one of the dramatic features of this beautiful stretch of coastline. The cliffs and rock stacks are composed of a pale ash and pumice from volcanic activity that occurred over seven million years ago.

18

Northland

19 Protected by the sand barrier of the Kaipara Heads, the tidal reaches of the **Kaipara Harbour** stretch from Helensville, near Auckland, north to Dargaville – a distance of almost 100 km. New Zealand's largest harbour, and one of the largest in the southern hemisphere, its many arms snake among low hills, creating an extensive shoreline.

20 Around 100,000 **bar-tailed godwits** (kuaka) and up to 70,000 knots (huahou) spend the summer in New Zealand where they fatten themselves up for the massive migration to their breeding grounds in northern Siberia and Alaska. Flocks of thousands can be seen on North Island estuaries, at high tide roosts such as this one at **Miranda** on the Firth of Thames.

The Volcanic Heart

In the dynamic central North Island the heat of the earth's interior surfaces to create places of great beauty but also at times immense destruction. The lakes and mountains resulting from this periodic upheaval are in many places surrounded by lush forests, while winter snows cap the highest volcanic peaks.

The Volcanic Heart

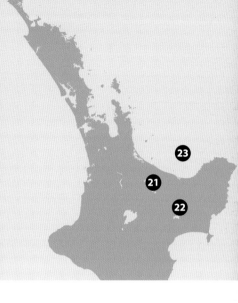

23 Stark and inhospitable, **White Island** or Whakari, is New Zealand's most active volcano. The main crater floor is only a few metres above sea level and is constantly changing due to ongoing activity. Located 48 km off Whakatane, it is part of a chain of active volcanoes running from the central North Island into the Pacific.

21 Rotorua's **Whakarewarewa** is the largest and best-known geyser field in New Zealand. The Pohutu Geyser, shown here, sends a jet of hot water 30 m skywards about 20 times a day.

22 Tree ferns are a striking feature of New Zealand's vegetation, conjuring up impressions of the time when dinosaurs walked the earth, especially in the primeval forests of **Urewera National Park**. The tallest of the tree ferns can reach 20 m in height, but the most recognised of them all is the ponga, or silver fern, worn proudly by New Zealand's sports representatives as an emblem of the country.

The Volcanic Heart

24 The New Zealand **weta**, a member of the grasshopper family, has undergone a bizarre spree of evolution, diverging into 100 or so species. From the long-legged cave weta to the giant weta, one of the world's heaviest insects, and to the fearsome tusked weta, these insects of the night occupy the most diverse range of habitats imaginable. One rare species of giant weta has found refuge in a patch of gorse in farmland at **Mahoenui** in the King Country. The area is now protected.

24

25

25 Although there are hot springs scattered all over New Zealand, the greatest concentration occurs around Rotorua and Taupo. This large spring, the **Champagne Pool** at **Waiotapu**, is 30 m across and lies over an explosion vent. The 'champagne' bubbles are carbon dioxide. Other trace minerals in the water produce the distinctive colourings.

26 Glow worms (titiwai) are the larvae of a small fly that uses light to attract its prey. At night they bring to life numerous shaded stream banks, but it is in the large limestone caves around the country, such as **Waitomo**, that they put on their most spectacular displays, covering the ceilings like the stars of the Milky Way.

26

27

27 Weighing just 6 g and a mere 8 cm in length, the tiny **rifleman** (titipounamu) is our smallest bird and is a member of the family of New Zealand wrens found nowhere else in the world. The high pitched staccato call of the rifleman is well known to trampers in more remote parts of the country, including the **Ureweras**.

28 New Zealand has many areas of limestone or karst country, including fields in Northland, Nelson, Paparoa and Fiordland. The action of water dissolving this rock carves entire underground river systems, many, such as these at **Waitomo**, embellished with long stalactites and stalagmites that have formed over the centuries, drop by drop.

28

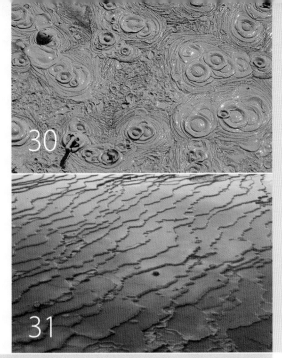

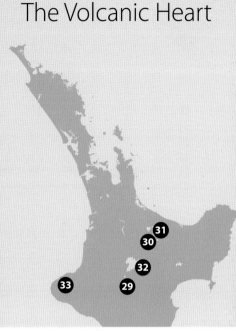

29 The eruption of **Mt Ruapehu** in 1995 and again in 1996 illustrates the dynamic forces still at work shaping New Zealand. Inactive since 1945, the mountain unexpectedly burst into life, sending columns of ash and steam high into the sky, spewing bombs of glowing lava and creating torrential mudflows.

30 Mud pools, such as these at **Orakei Korako**, form where acidic gas and steam make contact with the earth's surface beneath rainwater ponds. The surface rock is broken down to form clay particles and the resulting slurry of clay and water forms a very fine mud, which varies in viscosity depending on rainfall.

31 Thermal waters rising near the Champagne Pool at **Waiotapu** contain minerals that precipitate to form a deposit of sinter. These tiny **sinter terraces** replicate in miniature the grand Pink and White Terraces destroyed by the Tarawera eruption of 1886.

32 Lake Taupo is the result of the most violent volcanic eruption on earth in the last 5000 years. This blast ejected over 800 cubic kilometres of material, covering the country in ash and leaving a huge caldera in which the lake sits. The volcanic peaks of Tongariro National Park rise at the southern end of the lake.

33 Mt Taranaki/Mt Egmont is New Zealand's iconic volcanic cone, rising dramatically from rich forest and fertile farmland to a height of 2518 m. Last active over 350 years ago, the mountain offers many walks through diverse and botanically interesting terrain.

The Volcanic Heart

34 Tongaporutu River enters the Tasman Sea on a remarkable sweep of coastline where battered cliffs and rock stacks bear the brunt of the prevailing westerly winds. Away from the constantly shifting black sand beach and sand bars, low, windswept vegetation, common along the west coast of New Zealand, clings to the cliffs.

35 The haunting song of the **kokako**, also known as blue wattle crow, is seldom heard today outside reserves such as **Mapara** near Te Kuiti. This ancient member of the wattlebird family leaps through the forest canopy, making greater use of its legs than its limited powers of flight.

36

36 Reaching heights of up to
50 m, the **rimu** is among
New Zealand's tallest trees
and once graced lowland
forest throughout the country.
Whirinaki near Rotorua contains
wonderful stands of this graceful
giant, recognisable by its tall
slender trunk and the weeping
habit of its foliage.

37

37 Shortly after it leaves Lake Taupo, the Waikato River plunges through the thundering **Huka Falls** at a rate of 220,000 litres per second. New Zealand's longest river, at 435 km, the Waikato then winds its way north to the sea at Port Waikato, just south of Auckland.

38 Covered in winter snow are the three volcanic summits of Tongariro, Ngauruhoe and Ruapehu that make up the **Tongariro National Park**. Summer's heat melts the snow to reveal an arid scene of ash and rock expelled over the years from the periodically active craters.

38

37

38

39

39 The **Wanganui River** rises on the slopes of Mt Tongariro and flows through the remoteness of the stunning Whanganui National Park on its 329 km journey to the Tasman Sea. It is New Zealand's longest navigable river; canoeists can paddle for over 200 km through dramatic gorges and bush-clad riverbanks.

39

North to South

The spine of the North Island ranges peters out on the rugged Wellington coastline and dips into Cook Strait, the narrow but notoriously rough stretch of water dividing New Zealand into two main islands. South of the strait is a gentler coast of sunny beaches and deep, quiet inlets stretching inland to the beginnings of the Southern Alps.

41

40 Near the southern tip of the Wairarapa stand **Putangirua Pinnacles**, a fascinating maze of deep gullies and tall spires. The loose gravel conglomerate is easily eroded and the vertical funnelling of water has created a series of earth pillars protected by a cap of harder material.

42

41 Known as **orca**, or killer whale, these handsome marine mammals are often seen through the summer around Whangarei Harbour, the Hauraki Gulf and **Cook Strait**. Despite their name they are not whales but the largest member of the dolphin family, reaching up to 9 m in length.

42 The **tuatara** is an ancient reptile from the time of the dinosaurs now found only on protected conservation islands such as **Stephens Island**. Unique to New Zealand, it sits in an order of its own, Sphenodontia, one of the four orders into which all reptiles are placed.

43 Castle Point's 'castle' and 'reef', which enclose a sheltered bay, are composed of sandstone and siltstone that contain huge numbers of fossil shells. These are easily seen as they weather out of the soft rock, which is constantly buffeted by big seas on this exposed coast.

43

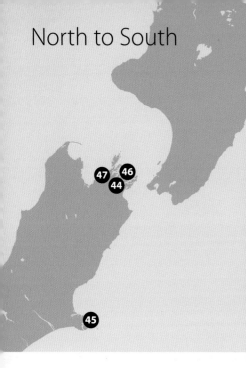

44 Pukeko are a ubiquitous part of the rural landscape and even make themselves at home in city parks and wetlands. Although found in other areas of the world, pukeko are considered an iconic New Zealand bird and their surprising powers of flight lead them to appear regularly on our offshore islands, including the many islands of the **Marlborough Sounds**.

45 A small area of **nikau palms** growing on **Banks Peninsula** near Akaroa are possibly the southernmost naturally growing palms in the world. Nikau is a feature tree in the coastal forest of the Heaphy Track and is an important food source for forest birds.

46 Maud Island frogs occupy coastal forest on the island of the same name in the Marlborough Sounds. Common among the New Zealand frogs is their primitive form of reproduction where the tadpole stage takes place inside the egg. A small froglet then hatches, so that standing water is not needed.

47 The beach at **Cable Bay** almost defies logic – the sea washes up against both sides of it. Connecting Pepin Island with the mainland beyond the bank is thrown up by the wave action of the open sea on the right, while to the left is a sheltered estuary wrapping around the island.

48 The South Island main divide reaches its northern limit among the beautiful scenery of the **Nelson Lakes** area. Sitting amidst 2000-m peaks, Lake Rotoiti lies just west of the divide and is drained by the mighty Buller River into the sea at Westport.

48

49 Divaricating plants, which produce tangles of intertwining twigs and branches, are uniquely prominent in the New Zealand flora, especially in the dry beech forests of the east coast of the South Island, such as at **Nelson Lakes**. One hypothesis suggests that they evolved as a protection against grazing by now extinct species of moa, giant birds which roamed New Zealand until the arrival of Maori.

50 Smallest of the penguins, the **blue penguin** (korora) is found all around the New Zealand coastline. Coastal communities, especially around the south coast of **Wellington**, may find a noisy pair of penguins setting up home under their floorboards.

49

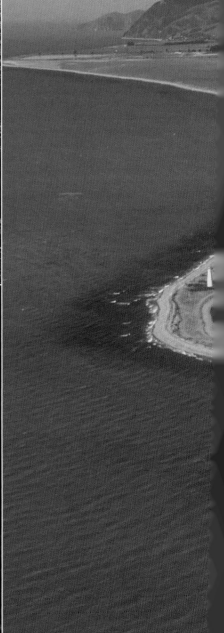

50

51 The **cabbage tree** (ti kouka) is a well loved part of New Zealand's rural landscape, including that around **Golden Bay** and Nelson. The largest member of the lily family, cabbage trees were valued by Maori for their fibrous leaves, used in weaving, and for their fleshy stems, which were cooked and eaten.

52 Creating a wonderful natural harbour for Nelson city, the 13-kilometre long **Nelson Boulder Bank** shelters the city from Tasman Bay. The boulders originate at MacKay Bluff in the distance, and become smaller and more rounded as they are pushed south by large seas.

51

52

53

54 With a length of 25 km, **Farewell Spit**, Onetahua, is the longest sandspit in the country. Arching gracefully off the northern tip of the South Island, with dunes up to 25 m high, the spit shelters the expanse of Golden Bay and provides a home for large numbers of migrant wading birds and a seasonal gannet colony.

54

53 Beech forests are very open, often with a moss-covered floor, giving them a fairyland quality. Found throughout the South Island (and the lower North Island above 300 m), they are a highlight of the road to Milford Sound, through the Haast Pass and the area around **Nelson Lakes**.

55 Abel Tasman National Park is a small gem. Its most obvious feature is the wonderful golden sand beaches, a product of the local geology. These are framed by rocky headlands behind which lies a very steep interior containing a wealth of botanical diversity.

55

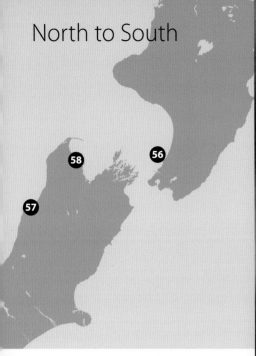

56

56 The New Zealand pigeon or **kereru** is a prolific feeder on forest fruits and is almost solely responsible for the seed distribution of many fruiting tree species. Found throughout the country, kereru are often heard before they are seen, given away by their noisy flight through the forest canopy. They are especially abundant on some offshore islands where bird sanctuaries have been established, such as Tiritiri Matangi and **Kapiti Island**.

57

57 From November to January, flowering **rata** are seen as splashes of red in the forest canopy, and are particularly showy here on the **West Coast** of the South Island. Rata often begin life as epiphytes perched high off the ground, eventually strangling their host trees to take their place in the forest.

58 Many of New Zealand's deepest and longest caves are to be found west of Nelson in the Mt Arthur and Takaka areas. The deepest caves drop to nearly 900m underground and stretch for 50km through hard limestone. **Harwood Hole**, New Zealand's deepest sinkhole at 172m, sits on the Takaka Hill near Abel Tasman National Park.

59 The drowned valleys of the **Marlborough Sounds** are a network of intricate waterways, islands and peninsulas popular for walking and boating. Tidal movements in the region reach an extreme at French Pass, where the peak flow creates a spectacle of swirling water, but other hidden corners provide tranquil retreats for tourists and wildlife.

60 The beautiful **Waikoropupu**, or Pupu Springs, is the largest of New Zealand's many freshwater springs,s and among the largest in the world. After years underground the water wells up crystal-clear at a rate of 14,000 litres per second.

60

Big Country

The collision of two plates in the earth's crust pushes the Southern Alps steadily upward while glaciers and large braided rivers relentlessly wear them down and carry the spoil away. East of the alps is dry open grassy country reaching to the coast, while to the west, lush rainforest enjoys a high rainfall from moisture-laden clouds coming in off the Tasman Sea.

61

63

63 The prominent ramparts of **Castle Hill** are hard to miss on the trip between Christchurch and Arthur's Pass. These limestone outcrops and boulders are eroded into a fascinating landscape, well known among the climbing fraternity for its superb rock routes and easy accessibility through farmland from the main road.

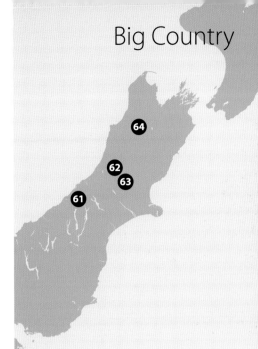

61 Tasman Glacier, flowing beneath the base of Mt Cook in the distance, is New Zealand's longest glacier at a length of 28.5 km. Like most glaciers around the world it is slowly receding, but it still carries vast amounts of rubble to the head of the Tasman River. Mt Cook climbs 2700 m directly from the glacier.

62 Notorious for its comic antics and the power of its dexterous beak, the **kea** is an inquisitive and intelligent alpine parrot that lives among the peaks of the Southern Alps. Kea make a regular appearance in alpine villages such as **Arthur's Pass** and on many ski fields, in search of food.

62

64

64 Maruia Falls came into existence when the powerful Murchison earthquake (7.8 on the Richter Scale) caused a rift in the riverbed in 1929. The power of the quake to create these 9-metre high falls gives an idea of the forces at work beneath the surface in a constantly changing New Zealand.

Big Country

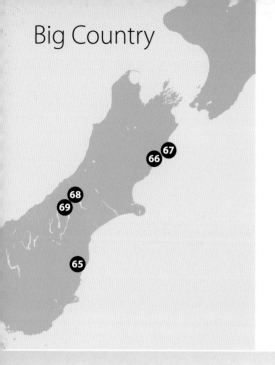

65 Yellow-eyed penguins, hoiho, are the largest of the three penguin species nesting on the mainland. These handsome birds nest among coastal vegetation between Banks Peninsula and Stewart Island and can be viewed returning to shore at such places as **Oamaru**. Hoiho dive to 160 m in search of the fish and squid that make up their diet.

66 Kaikoura Peninsula, known as the whale-watch capital of New Zealand, juts into the Pacific Ocean, while inland the snow-covered Kaikoura Ranges rise to over 2500 m. Nutrient-rich currents provide an abundance of year-round food in the coastal waters, supporting sperm whales, New Zealand fur seals, dolphins and many ocean-going bird species.

65

66

67 Herds of adolescent male **sperm whales**, the largest of the toothed whales, feed on giant squid in the depths of the **Kaikoura** Canyon. Just one among the 22 species of whale in New Zealand waters, sperm whales are often seen on the whale-watch tours for which Kaikoura is renowned.

68 Aoraki/ Mt Cook is New Zealand's highest peak at 3754 m. Of the 23 named peaks over 3000 m in New Zealand, all but one are inside the Mt Cook and neighbouring Westland national parks. Whether viewed from the rainforest of the West Coast or from the dry east, Mt Cook is an imposing sight.

69 The **Mt Cook lily** (a buttercup, in fact) is quite at home growing among the high snowy peaks of the Southern Alps. The largest of all buttercups, these delicate-looking flowers make a pre-Christmas show in alpine valleys such as the **Hooker Valley** at Mt Cook village, where they bloom against the stunning backdrop of Mt Cook.

Big Country

70 The continual rapid rise and erosion of the Southern Alps creates perfect conditions for magnificent **braided rivers** to form. While the confluence of the **Esk** and **Waimakariri** rivers is constrained by the foothills of the Southern Alps, on the Canterbury Plains these braided riverbeds can reach two to three kilometres or more in width.

71 Great spotted kiwi, the largest of the three kiwi species, are found only in the South Island in areas surrounding **Arthur's Pass**, Paparoa and Kahurangi national parks. This fascinating nocturnal bird emits an unearthly gruff call to announce its presence and will defend its territory with practised use of its strong legs and claws.

71

Big Country

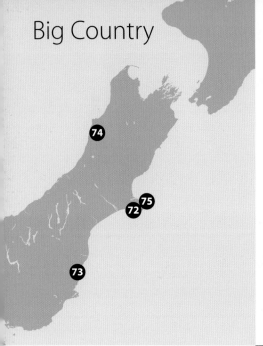

73 The **Moeraki boulders** are geological curiosities. Each boulder, up to 2 m across and weighing several tonnes, is a concretion that began 'growing' in sediments on the sea floor about 60 million years ago. Boulders can be seen peeling out of these sediments at the head of the beach.

72 Unlike geckos elsewhere in the world, the New Zealand species do not lay eggs but produce live young, usually twins. This rough and baggy-skinned **jewelled gecko** is one of over 60 species of lizard that, though rarely seen, occupy niches from isolated rocky coastlines, such as that on **Banks Peninsula**, to alpine herbfields.

72

73

74

74 Pancake Rocks is a promontory of limestone jutting into the Tasman Sea at Punakaiki. It has been eroded by wave action into a maze of caves, blowholes and the distinctive layered stacks from which it gets its name. The blowholes are at their most active at high tide.

75 The rare **Hector's dolphin**, tupoupou, at around 1.2 m long, is the world's smallest dolphin. It is frequently seen around **Banks Peninsula** and is easily identified by its rounded black dorsal fin – like a Mickey Mouse ear. An estimated 4000 Hector's dolphins remain, and there are only about 100 of the North Island sub-species, the Maui dolphin.

76 East of the Southern Alps a number of rivers and lakes exhibit a striking milky-blue colour as a result of their glacial origins. This is seen here in **Lake Pukaki** below the summit of Mt Cook. Very fine dust, produced by the slow grinding of glaciers over their rocky beds, hangs in the water to create this wonderful effect.

77 Many native species of tussock grassland once covered large areas of the South Island east of the Southern Alps. The rolling, snow-tussock covered hills of **Lindis Pass**, gateway south from the MacKenzie Country, present a well preserved and scenic example of this type of landscape.

78

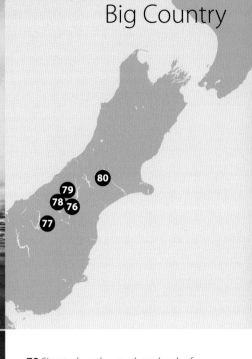

78 The **black stilt** (kaki) is an extremely rare wading bird, with a wild population of only about 150 birds. They are found almost exclusively in the wetlands and braided riverbeds of the **MacKenzie Basin**. Although a precarious habitat, the regular flooding of the riverbeds keeps the braids free of vegetation, allowing black stilts to nest and feed.

79

79 Situated on the northern bank of the Ahuriri River, the **Omarama clay cliffs** are an elegant series of ravines, ridges and pinnacles openly eroding to form 'badlands'. The sediments found in this formation react with the climate to create these distinctive clay cliffs.

80 The **wrybill** (ngutuparore) is a remarkable wading bird, unique in the world for its right-curving beak tip. Wrybill migrate within New Zealand, spending summers on the broad braided riverbeds of the South Island, such as the **Rakaia**, where they breed, and wintering on feeding grounds in the warmer North Island, such as Miranda on the Firth of Thames.

80

The Deep South

Glaciated valleys clothed in beech forest, deep cold lakes and swiftly flowing rivers create a wilderness playground. Along the coasts albatrosses, penguins and seals carry the flavour of the southern oceans, while gales frequently lash Stewart Island and the southern coastline.

The Deep South

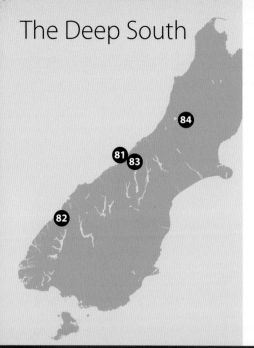

81 From its harsh beginning high on the Main Divide, **Franz Joseph Glacier** drops steeply to emerge in the lushness of the West Coast. Although generally in retreat, as most glaciers are around the world, the very high snowfall and speed of descent of this and the Fox Glacier allow them to advance again periodically.

82 Fiordland crested penguins breed only around the south-western coastline of New Zealand, where they are a regular sight for tour boat passengers cruising **Milford Sound**. Although ungainly as they leave the water and hop or waddle to their nests, their size and colouring make them a delight to watch.

82

83 Lying at an altitude of 2000 to 3000 m, this snowfield in the névé of **Fox Glacier** (to the left of Mount Tasman) receives large falls of snow which feed the famous glacier. New Zealand boasts a surprising 3144 glaciers that are more than 1 hectare in area, including several on Mt Ruapehu in the North Island.

84 Many forests of the central North Island and western South Island are dominated by an ancient lineage of conifer belonging to the family of podocarps. The seeds of these forest giants, such as this **kahikatea** at **Lake Brunner**, are, unusually, attached to the side of a fleshy fruit – a bounty of food for the birds that eat and disperse them.

83

84

85

86

86 The breeding colony of the **royal albatross** (toroa) at **Taiaroa Head**. This is one of the few places in the world where albatrosses breed on the mainland. These magnificent birds, which have a wingspan of 3 m, can live for 50 years and cover thousands of kilometres of the southern oceans in their search for food.

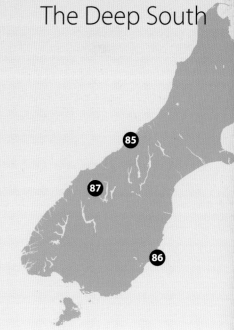

85 Known for the stunning views of Mt Cook reflected on its surface, **Lake Matheson** is a kettle lake formed 14,000 years ago at the retreat of the last ice age. Kettle lakes are created by partially buried blocks of ice left behind as the glaciers recede and the resulting hollows remain filled with water.

87 At 3030 m, **Mt Aspiring** is the only peak over 3000 m that lies outside the Mt Cook area; it is located 130 km to the south in Mt Aspiring National Park. A favourite among mountaineers, the pyramid-like horn of Mt Aspiring is also a familiar backdrop for the large number of trampers and skiers who use the park.

87

The Deep South

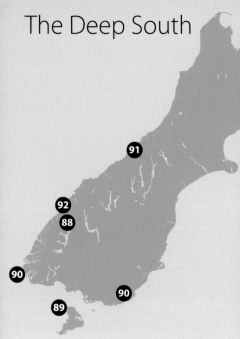

88 Among the highest waterfalls in the world, and certainly New Zealand's highest, the **Sutherland Falls** are a popular sight on the famous Milford Track. From Lake Quill the falls drop 580 m, in three stages, into the Arthur River, which goes on to flow into Milford Sound.

89 The **kakapo**, seen here on **Codfish Island**, is the world's heaviest and only flightless parrot. Its nocturnal and solitary lifestyle is also unusual, and unique in New Zealand is its use of a lek mating system, where a male sits in a manicured 'track and bowl' system, and calls to attract a mate.

90 Once considered an unusual sight, New Zealand **fur seals**, or kekeno, are increasing their breeding range around the South Island and lower North Island and becoming more numerous. There are a number of breeding grounds around the coast of **Otago** and **Fiordland**, and although the pungent smell of these colonies is off-putting, the antics of the seals can be very entertaining.

91 While in no way unique to New Zealand, the white heron or **kotuku** is well known and loved in this country despite a low population of little over 100 birds. From the breeding colony at **Okarito** in Westland, herons disperse widely and may be seen on estuaries and wetlands around New Zealand.

92 Mitre Peak rises dramatically to a jagged summit 1692 m above the waters of Milford Sound. Large waterfalls spill from these mountains during the frequent heavy rains. Carved by glaciers, the steep sides of the fiord loom ominously above the many boats that ply its sheltered waters.

93

95

96

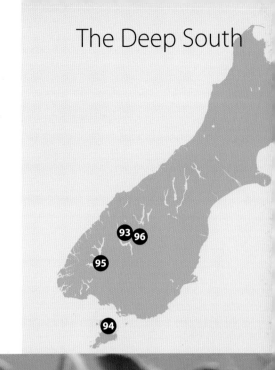

93 In this scene near Queenstown, the **Shotover River** joins the **Kawarau River** shortly after the latter leaves **Lake Wakatipu**. This is a landscape shaped by glaciers, which have ground away the bedrock and smoothed the flanks of the surrounding mountains, leaving low rounded hills in the foreground that proved more resistant to the great weight of ice.

94 Kaka, the large forest parrot, is found throughout New Zealand but is relatively uncommon. They are most often seen on islands, such as **Stewart Island** where they appear around Oban township feeding playfully in the treetops and occasionally flashing the bright red feathers they hide under their wings.

94

95 Thought for many years to be extinct, the **takahe** was rediscovered in the mountains of Fiordland west of **Lake Te Anau** in 1948. From a population of little more than 100, this large flightless bird is making a comeback and there are now small populations at sanctuaries around the country.

96 Lake Wakatipu, the longest lake in New Zealand, nestles in an alpine wonderland with the popular resort of Queenstown on its northern shore and the magnificent **Remarkables** mountains flanking its eastern shores. Its tributary valleys offer great walking opportunities and are a gateway to both the Mt Aspiring and Fiordland national parks.

The Deep South

97 The Catlins coast has some of the most fossil-rich rock in New Zealand. As the tide recedes at **Curio Bay**, the fossilised remains of a forest that lived about 180 million years ago become exposed. A very detailed record of the trees that once grew here is recorded in stone on this exposed rock platform.

98 Hooker's sea lions breed in large colonies on the Auckland and Campbell Islands in New Zealand's southern waters but are also regular visitors to the **Southland** coast. This is a much larger animal than the fur seal but smaller than the elephant seal, which occasionally appears on New Zealand beaches.

97

98

99

99 Blue ducks, whio, are at home in fast-moving forest rivers and streams, where they dabble and dive for aquatic invertebrates such as the caddisfly larvae. Though uncommon, they are still widespread on many wilderness rivers from the central North Island south, including the **Hollyford River** in Fiordland.

100

100 The **Buller's albatross** is one of about 60 species of albatrosses, petrels, shearwaters and other seabirds recorded in New Zealand waters, making pelagic birdwatching very popular, especially around the southernmost coast of New Zealand and **Stewart Island**.

PHOTOGRAPHIC CREDITS:

The publishers acknowledge the following photographic libraries
and individual photographers whose work is reproduced in this book.
Photographs are numbered consecutively through the book. Where the
photograph is not numbered, a page reference is given.

Robin Bush: 20, 27; Richard Chambers: 38; Focus New Zealand Photo
Library: 11, 16, 19, 32, 36, 39, 87; Mark Jones: 1, 4, 65, 69, 99; Department
of Conservation, Tony Lilleby: 17; Natural Sciences Image Library (NSIL):
pages 3, 4, 7 (left), 22–23, 48–49, 60–61; pictures 7, 8, 12, 21, 23, 28, 31, 33,
34, 35, 37, 40, 42, 43, 44, 45, 46, 47, 48, 49, 50, 52, 54, 56, 57, 58, 60, 61, 62,
63, 64, 66, 68, 70, 72, 73, 75, 77, 80, 81, 83, 84, 85, 86, 88, 90, 91, 93, 94, 95,
96, 97, 98; Northland NZ.com: 2, 6; Krzystof Pfeiffer: 25; PhotoNewZealand:
9 (Paul Kennedy), 53 (Belinda Pope); Tui de Roy: 3, 10, 15, 18, 22, 24, 29, 30,
41, 51, 55, 67, 71, 76, 78, 82, 89, 100; Shutterstock: 5 (Thomas Nord), pages
34–35, 59 (Holger Mette), page 7 (right), 74 (4139979233), 76 (Douglas
Lichfield), 92 (Stuart Taylor); and Rafael Valentino: 14, 79.